How Tony 1

Growing up Dyslexic

My name is Tony.

When I graduated from preschool, all the kids knew the alphabet but me.

When I was 8 years old and still couldn't read or write, my mother took me to a neurologist. After many tests, he said,

"Tony, "You are severely dyslexic.

You might never read or write."

Mom and I wrote this book to tell you how it feels to be the only kid in my class who couldn't read.

I needed my mother's help. In high school, college and grad school, I needed her help. I worked hard and never gave up.

my high school graduation

Finally, I taught myself to read.

This is my story. I hope it will help others who are growing up dyslexic. or who have children with dyslexia.

This book is dedicated to

Bob, Shanna, Thamora, Oren, Damian, Aiden, Virginia, Mrs. Levesque.

To students with dyslexia and to families everywhere who are trying to understand how to help their dyslexic children

Published in 2021
by Flying Heron Books
516 SW North River Point Drive, Stuart Florida 34994
For Permissions-For information on bulk purchases
Contact Judy Fishel jjfishel@gmail.com

Cover picture is a stock photo Other pictures taken by Tony's parents
Library of Congress Control Number 2020915396
Publisher's Cataloging-in-Publication Data provided by Five Rainbows Cataloging Services

Names: Fishel, Tony, author. | Fishel, Judy, author.

Title: How Tony learned to read: growing up dyslexic/ by Tony Fishel and Judy Fishel.

Description: Stuart, FL: Flying Heron Books, 2021.

Identifiers: LCCN 2020915396(print)
ISBN 978-0-9906112-7-1(paperback)
ISBN 978-0-9906112-8-8(ebook)
ISBN 978-0-9906112-9-5(audiobook)

Subjects: LCSH: Dyslexics--Biography.

Dyslexic children. |Dyslexia. | Learning disabilities--Biography. |Mothers and sons. | Reading, Psychology of. | Reading. | BISAC: FAMILY & RELATIONSHIPS / Learning Disabilities. | EDUCATION / Special Education / Learning Disabilities. | LANGUAGE   ARTS & DISCIPLINES / Reading Skills.

Classification: LCC LB1050.5.F572020(print) | LCC LB1050.5(ebook) | DDC 371.91/44--dc23.

"It is the loneliness and the feeling of isolation that is the worst part."

TONY FISHEL

Table of Contents

Introduction

This book is Tony's Story told from two points of view. Tony tells the story as he experienced it.

His mother, Judy, tells Tony's Story as she experienced it.

They share the stories from both points of view to help both parents and students with dyslexia understand:

- what it feels like to be dyslexic.

- what it's like when everyone else in your class thinks you are stupid.

- how important it is to feel good about yourself.

- the importance of having parents and children try to understand each other.

- and how, most of all, when nothing seemed to help, one determined boy taught himself to read.

You might notice that we are using the font, Comic Sans MS, for Tony's reflections. Of the commonly used fonts, this seems to be easiest for people with dyslexia to read. It is used in this paragraph.

Tony's Mother, Judy, uses Ariel.

The narrator uses Times New Roman.

We use slightly larger fonts than usual and leave more space between lines to make it easier to read.

Note to Readers

Occasionally we include comments or suggestions you might find helpful.

Students: the person (of any age) with dyslexia.

Parents: includes parents, grandparents, teachers, caregivers, and anyone else who is trying to help the student.

When Tony and Judy first discussed this book, they both pictured a 'feel-good' book saying:

"Tony has dyslexia. He was told 'You might never learn to read or write'. He kept working. Finally, he taught himself to read."

As Tony began writing, his image of the book was not so cheerful. He remembered how it felt to be the only kid in his class who couldn't read.

In this book, Tony shares the pain of growing up dyslexic, the pain he never shared with his parents when he was a child, the pain that has never gone away.

Tony and Judy hope that their failures and successes will help you find your way.

They hope you will discover ways to help you deal with your problems.

And students, they hope this book helps you as you are growing up dyslexic.

Chapter 1.

Tony's First Five Years

In the Philippines

Tony was born Manilla, January 30,
1972. His family included his parents,
Bob and Judy Fishel, and his five-year old
sister, Thamora.

They were living in the Philippines,
working with a group that did demonstration
community development projects. This part
of the story is important for two reasons.

Years later, when Tony was tested by
the school system in Massachusetts, the
"experts" tried very hard to explain why
Tony was having "reading problems." Most
of their explanations were based on these
early experiences.

There were also experiences in these early
years showing that Tony was unusually

intelligent. These helped his family ignore
the "experts" when they said things like
"Boys learn more slowly than girls" or
"Some boys just have trouble learning to
read. Give him time."

Tony was born nearly one month late. The
doctor, of course, explained that his mother
hadn't counted right but Tony was big at 8½
pounds. Years later, the "experts" wondered
if his late birth caused his reading problems.

Because both of his parents were working,
they had a wonderful Filipino woman, Flora,
who lived with them and took care of Tony.

Flora spoke to him in Filipino, her assistant
spoke Cebuano (from a Southern Island)
and Tony's family spoke English. Tony
constantly heard three languages. Because
he spent more time with Flora at that time,
he understood more Filipino.

Thamora was already fairly fluent in Filipino
and sometimes explained to Tony what their
parents were saying.

His parents agreed with many other people that learning several languages when you are young is helpful. The "experts," however, decided this must have caused Tony's reading problems.

Tony was walking at seven months. Soon he was running and climbing up the stairs. Certainly, this did not cause his reading problems

Judy was an Assistant Principal at the International School. The elementary school had just hired their first special education teacher. She told Judy about dyslexia and asked her to be alert to students with certain problems.

Later on, this helped Judy recognize and understand dyslexia when Tony began showing some of these problems.

The Marshall Islands

When Tony was two-and-a-half years old, his family moved to the Marshall Islands. These islands are in the Pacific Ocean about half-way between Hawaii and Guam. They cover a million square miles of ocean but there are only seventy square miles of land spread out over the 29 atolls.

Tony

My first memories are from the time we lived in the Marshall Islands. With my blond hair, I looked a little different from the Marshallese boys but I was treated the same. I don't remember feeling that much different.

I spent my time walking barefoot on the reefs, exploring tide pools and catching fish with my bare hands just like everyone else my age. I also learned to climb — at least half-way up a coconut palm.

Judy

One of my most vivid memories of Tony was when he was four years old. He counted to 14 but then he counted 14, 14, 14, 14, 20. His counting skills were not great, but his math concepts were amazing.

One morning when I went to wake him up, Tony asked "Mommy, how much is 100 plus 100?"

I was astonished. I didn't think Tony knew what a hundred was. I asked if he'd been dreaming about numbers. Tony was insistent.

"Yes," I said."100 plus 100 is 200.

Tony continued "Does this mean 200 plus 200 is 400?" We never learned how he had known about addition.

Later, Tony asked a common question, "What is the biggest number?"

We explained that there wasn't a "biggest number." If you said one billion, someone could say one billion and one. We explained that numbers were infinite; they went on and on forever.

Most kids stop here, deciding this is more than they want to know, but Tony kept thinking. He knew there was no way to count every hair on your head or every drop of water in the ocean but he understood that they still were not infinite.

Preschool

One of the group's projects was starting a preschool. Tony was 4 years old when he went to the first Marshallese preschool. One day Tony came home all excited.

"Today, we learned the last letter of the alphabet."

"That's great," his mother said. "What was the letter?" Tony had no idea. He thought it had something to do with a Zebra.

They taught the children all the letters of the alphabet, but Tony didn't know any of them.

Now, remembering the special ed teacher in the Philippines, his mother wondered if Tony might be dyslexic.

Parents: This should have been a clear sign that Tony might be dyslexic. I should have begun then, helping him learn the letters of the alphabet. I assumed he would learn them in Kindergarten but I was wrong.

Buy Alphabet books. Ask what the letters look like. Teach your child that letters have names. Start with the child's name or words they choose. Learn the names and sounds of these letters. Make this fun not work.

Read to your children. Read their favorite books over and over. You want them to enjoy books and look forward to learning to read.

Tony

I have a clear memory of being in preschool where, one day, I picked up a coconut crab. I was with other kids when we found it near the preschool. I had learned from the neighborhood boys how to grab and hold large crabs but I had never seen a coconut crab before.

This crab didn't seem that dangerous so, with each of the big snapping claws firmly held in my hands, I proudly brought it over to some of the teachers. Instead of being impressed, they freaked out. They were concerned that I would get my fingers snapped off. I had no idea that a crab could be so dangerous.

Tony's Dream

The first dream Tony remembers is related to a place where they often went swimming. Sand that had been dredged formed a pile that must have been 20-30 feet high.

They often laughed and called it Sand Mountain, the highest point in the Marshall Islands. The water around it was shallow and calm. It was a nice place for children to play.

Tony

I remember the ocean, the sand, and isolation. I liked being at the beach but I was afraid because I couldn't swim and, for some reason, I was afraid of the large pile of sand. I was also afraid of the older children.

The first dream I remember was one I had when we lived in the Marshalls. I dreamt of being on a small home-made raft out at sea.

I was in the trough between the waves and they were big, so big that I could not see Majuro.

I felt afraid but I knew that, as the wave passed, the raft and I would be buoyed up and, from the crest, I would see Majuro. But, as I rose to the top of the wave, all I could see were more waves in every direction.

I'm not sure if I passed out or how I got there but the next thing I remember was being on the giant sand dune on Majuro, the one that they made when they dredged out the channel for the big ships to be able to refuel.

I'm on that mountain of sand and I expect to see the island and our little group of homes but again, when I get to the top, it's not what I expect.

I am not just a short walk from home. I am on top of a sand dune in a desert. Before, all I saw were waves Now, all I could see were waves of sand.

Judy

It is strange that Tony was afraid of that beach. He and the other children of people on our staff never went there without me or another adult.

I was surprised when Tony wrote about his dream. I considered leaving it out. It had nothing to do with dyslexia. But, as we continued working, Tony referred to that dream several times. To him, it was important.

Tony

Another of my strongest, most lasting memories was when my parents were away for a few days, leaving me with friends. I missed them terribly. I thought it was my heart that hurt so bad. That made sense to me.

Then, for some reason, the roof of my mouth hurt. I remember thinking that didn't make any sense. For many years, when I was homesick, I felt that same pain in the roof of my mouth.

Judy

At first, I had no idea what Tony was talking about. Finally, I remembered taking a group of kids in fourth to sixth grade on a copra ship. The ship went from one atoll to another collecting copra (dried coconut) and trading for food. It gave us a look at the outer islands.

We were gone six to eight days. Thamora was with me on the boat. I have no memory of Bob being away but I wouldn't be surprised.

The families we worked with would take care of Tony just as we would care for their children if they were away.

I had no idea this upset Tony so much. He might have said "I missed you Mommy," but I don't think he ever told us how terribly he missed me.

Chapter 2.

Back to the United States

Tony's family left the Marshall Islands when he was five. Their first stop was in Hawaii where, at the airport, Tony was introduced to escalators and the elevator. When the elevator door opened, Tony thought this was a hotel room. He'd heard of hotels but had never been in one.

When the elevator opened on another floor, Tony was amazed. "How'd you do that?" he asked, thinking his father had somehow changed the scenery.

The next stop was San Francisco. Here Tony saw his first tall buildings and he had trouble understanding the "people" he saw in store windows.

He continually said things like "There sure are big buildings on this island." It was hard to explain why this wasn't an island and why he couldn't find the ocean.

The third stop was in Chicago, the headquarters for the organization Tony's parents worked with. Because adults would be in all day meetings, the children all went to a summer camp only for children of families that worked with us.

For Tony, this was not a happy experience. He was one of the youngest kids. He was away from his parents and, unlike the other children, he didn't know anyone there except his sister.

Tony

To say that it was not a happy experience might be a euphemism. I don't have any positive memories of that camp other than my sister. We were apart most of the day. At meals and sometimes at the waterfront, we would see and talk to each other.

I remember telling her how terrible it all was. I remember Thamora's sadness she had when she saw me with a real bad black eye. I had tripped and hit the bricks next to the fireplace in the cabin.

Looking back, that was the first time I remember Thamora caring about me and being there for me.

This was one of the most terrible experiences in my life. I felt profoundly anxious. The only person I trusted was my sister. She had a good time but I felt abandoned.

This was the first place I felt that other people were out to get me, that they were not to be trusted, that I was different. I even felt that some of the kids were evil.

Judy

I knew this would be hard for Tony at first. Thamora knew some of the girls and she made new friends quickly. When she realized how upset Tony was, she tried to spend time with him and comfort him. If I had known this would be such a traumatic experience for Tony, I would certainly have tried to keep him home.

An Interesting Question

Did these difficult events, his fear of Sand Mountain, missing his mother when she was away, or being at camp cause Tony to have similar fears later? Perhaps Tony began to connect new difficulties with past fears. However, it seems unlikely that his early fears could have caused his dyslexia or affected his reading in any way.

Davis, California and Kindergarten

While Bob spent the year leading training schools in India, Korea, Jamaica, and Venezuela, the rest of the family spent the year in Davis, California.

Thamora was in sixth grade. It was her first experience in an American school. Tony was in kindergarten. Both seemed happy. There were no clues that Tony might be dyslexic.

They took several trips to National Parks and once drove up into mountains to see snow. Each person had a bicycle and used them to explore the parks in the area.

Tony

The main thing I remember about Davis was these two foster kids. I was afraid of them.

As I write this, I question how much of this was only in my head. My lens of insecurity can turn any normal healthy interaction into a twisted image.

Judy

This was a shock. At first, I didn't know what Tony was talking about. These were two little boys Tony's age or younger that lived in some sort of foster care facility.

I needed to use every chance I could to earn a little extra to help pay the bills. I got about $20 a week for two hours with the two boys. I could take my children along. We did things like going to the Zoo or to a playground.

I'm sure I explained to my children why we were doing this. It was both to give the boys a chance to have some fun and to help us earn some extra money. Neither of my children objected then. I think Tony must have associated them with the boys in summer camp.

The Microscope

We visited my parents before moving to California. When we left them, I took an old microscope I'd been given when I was young. I thought I'd have time to use it myself, or that Thamora would be interested.

But no, it became Tony's microscope. On his way home from kindergarten, he collected bits and pieces to look at. When possible, he found something to hold water and collected pond water I would get home to find Tony at the kitchen table, with his assorted samples on glass slides. He'd urge me to come look at what he'd found.

Again, I felt certain that Tony was an amazing child, that I didn't need to worry about him. He was sure to do well in school.

I wonder why Tony remembers a few hours having fun with two boys but he never mentioned time spent using the microscope.

Parents: Again, I was too trusting. I assumed that Tony's kindergarten teacher would let me know if Tony hadn't learned his letters. I should have been sure.

Before kindergarten, children should know many letters. When they finish, they should know all letters with upper and lower cases (Aa) and understand that letters were associated with sounds. They should also be able to write their name.

Chapter 3.

First Grade in Brockton MA

At the end of the year in California, Judy and the children joined Bob in Guatemala to help with a workshop in a small village.

Then they went to Brockton, MA where Bob began work as the pastor of a small United Methodist Church. Thamora was in seventh grade. Tony was in first grade.

Tony seemed happy enough in first grade but it soon was obvious that he was reversing many of his letters. This was accepted as normal in kindergarten but not in first grade. His mother tried helping him but had no success.

His teacher said they shouldn't worry, that he would outgrow this soon enough.

Judy

One of my favorite memories from that year was meeting Tony's first grade teacher. She told me this story.

She had asked the students to give examples of words starting with the c/k sound. Because they had practiced this before, most of the children repeated words they had learned in class: C is for cat, candy, cake, etc.

Tony's contribution was original. "C is for compost pile." The other children were sure he was wrong. "That's not a word." "You made that up."

I suspect they thought they were supposed to name only words they had heard in class. The teacher, however, thought it was a great answer.

She asked Tony if he would like to tell the class what a compost pile was. So, Tony explained why compost piles were helpful and then described how to build one.

His teacher also assured us that Tony was reading very well and that "unlike the other children, Tony read with such expression."

At the end of the year, Tony came home with a class picture. A few days later, he tore the picture into little pieces left on the floor. We didn't really understand why.

Tony

My understanding was that I really could read but I knew it wasn't the way the other kids read. Somehow, they all knew a secret method that I never understood.

My system for reading was to listen carefully when the other kids read so I would understand the story. I might look at the first several letters or even the first letters of several words. When I had an idea how the sentence started, I'd predict the rest of the sentence based on what I knew about the story and sometimes based on the pictures.

This wasn't fake reading. This was the way I read. When the teacher said I read well, I knew it was a good method even if I didn't know the secret method.

Parents: We knew Tony wasn't reading. We sometimes said he could have "read" just as well with the book upside down or on the wrong page. We did not realize that he still didn't know his letters.

What we should have done was have him tested right away. The earlier dyslexia is identified, the easier it is to help the child. If the school doesn't help, look for a pediatric neurologist. You might also try some of the materials for helping dyslexic children on the Internet.

The Summer after First Grade

It was that summer when Tony tried reading some familiar signs. He asked "What is N-K-B-O… His mother was confused. No signs she could see included those letters. Finally, she figured it out.

It was hard to believe that Tony couldn't recognize the letters. The letters he was looking at were MCDO. You might recognize it better with a lower-case c.

Later, she tested Tony's ability to recognize other letters and was shocked. Sometimes he guessed right but most of the time he was wrong.

She handed him a copy of *Hop on Pop*, not realizing that this was one of the most difficult books to read for someone who is dyslexic. Tony tried to guess at some of the words but clearly could not read any of them.

She then borrowed some very simple pre-primers from a kindergarten teacher she knew. She and Tony spent several hours a day all summer working on letters, sounds, and simple reading.

Judy

I was a teacher. I'd even taken a class on teaching reading. I kept thinking I should be able to teach Tony to read. When he showed no improvement, I felt like I was the one who had failed, not Tony.

Just before school started, we went to talk to the principal. We wanted Tony tested for dyslexia and also wanted him to repeat first grade. (We discussed this with Tony first and he had agreed that this might be a good idea.)

The Testing

Massachusetts had a reputation for being really good about helping children with learning problems so Bob and Judy trusted those doing the tests. The testing seemed quite thorough. Tony took one test after another for about a week.

One test involved copying shapes, some quite difficult. There were also letters of the alphabet. Tony did well with the shapes but had problems with the letters.

Another part of the testing involved an interview with the parents. This is where the "experts" asked about Tony's early experiences and came to the conclusions that Tony's reading problems must have been caused by his learning several languages at the same time, or because he was born late. They also insisted that Tony was much too young to test for dyslexia. Now we know that wasn't true.

Tony

I only have a vague memory of those tests. I now understood that I confused letters like b and d, p and q. It was hard for me but it really didn't seem like a big problem. I still thought I was reading well enough even though I used a different method.

When my parents suggested that I repeat first grade, that was OK with me. I thought it might help me learn the secret.

Judy

When Bob and I went to a meeting at Tony's school to learn the results of the testing. It certainly wasn't what we had expected.

They explained that, even if our daughter had no problems learning to read, we should not expect our son to learn as quickly because **boys learn more slowly than girls.** They also explained that **Tony was a slow learner.**

We knew they were wrong. Tony was not a slow learner. But it was not easy to disagree with "experts" who had just spent a week testing our son. We just hoped that, with a second year of first grade, Tony would catch up.

We should have taken Tony to a neurologist.

We now understand it was not unusual for the "experts" working for the school department to avoid saying the child needed special help. They down-play the child's problems so the schools would not be required to offer special services.

Parents: Remember that none of this happened recently. It was over 40 years ago. Yet, even now, there are many teachers and others in the school system who are not aware of dyslexia. They don't realize that children like Tony should be tested as early as possible.

In better school systems today, you might find well trained staff to help your student. They will also be able to suggest qualified neurologists and others trained to help students like yours.

We were still depending on the teachers to teach Tony to read but now I don't think his teachers had any idea how to do this.

Today parents can use a computer to search for programs that claim to help dyslexic students. There are many such programs. You might try several of these programs to see if any seem helpful for your child.

By now, Tony should have learned simple and some complex letter sounds. (the sounds for B or F or T – and for Br, or Ch, or Thr. First graders should know sounds of the letters and read simple books. Tony was way behind.

Chapter 4.

First Grade and Second Grade

After the first month of repeating first grade, Tony's teacher said she'd like him in math with the second graders.

This sounded good but later his parents looked back and asked themselves how they could have been so stupid. They should have asked questions. They should have asked about his reading.

Judy

A month went by before we learned that second graders had math while first graders had reading. While his class was doing math, the teacher gave Tony reading worksheets.

We were furious but knew it was partly our fault. We should have talked to the teachers more often about Tony's reading.

The principal suggested we move Tony back to second grade. He could go to a reading specialist every day. This seemed like a good plan, though we wished they had suggested it earlier.

After a few weeks we talked to the reading teacher. She explained that she rarely had time with Tony because she had so many other students in her class all at the same time, all with different problems.

Tony

I don't remember caring if I was in first or second grade. I do remember feeling isolated. I never seemed to fit in. The other kids didn't tease me or bully me, but they occasionally laughed at me like the time I asked someone how to spell "us." Sometimes I felt like everything I did was probably going to be wrong.

I never had friends that went to my school. I'm not sure why. It might have been that they didn't want a friend who couldn't read.

Maybe I just didn't know how to make friends. I had friends from the neighborhood and my best friend was a boy in our church.

I remember having many fears. I was afraid of being abandoned and afraid of older children.

I was especially afraid of teenagers I'd been told were out in the woods where I often played. I'd never seen them but I had heard they were out there in the woods smoking pot.

I couldn't imagine how they could smoke a pot and that made it even more scary.

Judy

Tony began sleep-walking. He'd get up at night, go out the door, and start walking toward his school. This continued through seventh grade.

There were several hopeful signs that year. One student in Tony's class asked the teacher why it was hot in the summer and cold in winter.

The teacher said "It is hot in the summer because the earth is closer to the sun. In the winter we are farther away from the sun." It sounds perfectly logical, doesn't it?

Tony raised his hand and said politely "Actually, it's the other way around. We are closer to the sun in the winter and farther away in the summer."

The teacher asked if he'd like to go to the library to find an encyclopedia. He said no, he would bring his encyclopedia from home. How could he use the library encyclopedia? He couldn't read.

We were surprised to discover Tony knew this. He learned it watching science programs on TV. The temperature on the earth is related to the tilt of the earth, not the distance from the sun.

The next day, the teacher let Tony explain to the class what he had learned, and even better, she thanked Tony for correcting her mistake.

Another memorable event took place in church. During the sermon, Tony grabbed my arm and whispered "Mom, did you know that six times seven is the same as seven times six? Tony hadn't started multiplication in school.

"Yes," I whispered. "I know that. How did you know?"

Tony pointed to the church windows with six panes across and seven panes up and down. He explained how six sevens and seven sixes made the same number. It was great to know Tony was still exploring math concepts on his own.

Parents: Ask your child regularly about how school is going – what's easy, what's hard, how they're feeling, if they have any problems, and if you can help.

Never push your child to try harder. They are already trying harder. Accept them. Encourage them. Love them just the way they are.

I read an article by Emily Hanford. www. ampreports.org/episode/2019/08/22/what's -wrong-with-how-schools-teach-reading?

According to the article, most schools today are using the worst possible method of teaching reading: the three-cue system. It involves looking at the pictures and guessing what the word is. It also suggests that students ask if the word looks right and sounds right. This method is commonly used by poor readers.

Another method is phonics. It's important to use phonics but you cannot learn to read only by sounding out all the words.

Whole language focuses on learning to recognize the whole word. This is what the best readers do but they still need strategies to use for words they haven't learned.

The best system is a combination. Children need phonics to sound out words they don't know. They also need to understand the structure of our language. Many words cannot be understood by sounding them out like: night, light, and sight.

Students need vocabulary so they know the meaning of the words. Finally, they need Visual Memory or word recognition so after they learn a word, they will know it when they see it again.

Judy

If I had known this forty years ago, I might have been able to help Tony learn to read.

Finding a dyslexia tutor or therapist

If these wonderful people existed 40 years ago, no one told me about it. Now you can check your computer and search for "find a dyslexia tutor" and you'll find a list of those in your area. They also offer online programs

You want someone trained in the Orton Gillingham system and maybe Lindamood, Wilson, MSLE systems, someone who works mainly with dyslexic students at the age of your child.

They often charge $25-$100 or more per hour. This is sometimes covered partially or completely by insurance. Use your computer to learn about free programs or programs you can use yourself. I'd suggest starting as early as possible.

Chapter 5.

Third Grade and More Testing

Tony finished second grade, still not able to read or write. When he began third grade, his parents requested that he be tested again.

The "experts" went through another week of testing. This time, there were more people in the group that gave them the results. His parents will never forget the conclusion of these "experts." One of the men stood and said firmly:

"Tony's only problem is that he has a pushy mother."

As Judy said later, "I was pushing them to help Tony. I was not pushing my son. It would have done no good to respond and tell them they were wrong. Obviously, they had no plans to help Tony learn to read.

As they left the room, one woman who stayed behind spoke to them "Don't you believe that nonsense," she said. "What you need to do is take that boy of yours to a neurologist.

"Then, when you get a paper saying that your boy needs to be in a special class for dyslexic students, you take that paper to the school superintendent.

"The superintendent will tell you they have a program for students who have dyslexia but it's full; He will put your boy on a waiting list. Tell him it's against the law to put a child on a waiting list.

"The superintendent knows that but he will be surprised to learn that you know. It might take a week or two but they will place your boy in a special class. It's a small class with only seven or eight students and a teacher trained to help dyslexic students.

"If anyone can teach your boy how to read, she's the one who can do it."

That afternoon, Judy called a neurologist in Boston. The usual time for an appointment was 2-3 months but they had just gotten a cancellation. Could she bring him the next morning? Of course, she could.

Judy

I sat silently in the back of the room until the testing was over. This was about forty years ago so I don't remember very much but two tests stick in my memory.

The neurologist gave Tony a subtraction problem. It was something like $3602 - 824$. Tony looked at it carefully, closed his eyes, and then answered. The neurologist was shocked. Tony was correct. I was shocked.

As far as I know, no one had taught Tony to do math in his head. Tony was then asked to show his work on the paper. He gave it a good try but, as usual, he confused left and right. He borrowed from the left one time and then from the right. He crossed out things and tried again. He knew the answer but could not get the answer on paper.

In one test, the neurologist had a book. On one side were perhaps six shapes, all different, each with a different pattern.

On the other side was a single pattern. Tony needed to find the one shape matching both the shape and the pattern. Each time the page was turned there was another similar problem.

Tony understood what he was to do right away. Quickly, he'd point to his answer. The neurologist suggested that Tony slow down. There wasn't any hurry. But Tony knew he could do this. He went faster and faster as if it was a game.

Sometimes the neurologist asked Tony to explain why he chose a certain response. Tony had no problem with this. I was pretty sure he got every single one correct.

Most people taking this test would have taken their time double-checking their responses. Tony never explained why he went so fast. Maybe he was just having fun. Maybe he wanted the neurologist to know that he wasn't dumb.

After two hours of interesting tests, the neurologist turned to Tony who was only eight years old and said very seriously,

"Tony, you are incredibly intelligent, not just in the top one percent but in the top half of one percent. You are also severely dyslexic. You might never learn to read or write."

Finally, I asked a question. "You said Tony **might** never learn to read or write. Does this mean that he still **might** learn to read and write?"

"Yes," he said. "Some people who are severely dyslexic do learn to read and write but we cannot say what makes the difference between those who do and those who don't. All I can say, Tony, is work hard and give it your best try."

The Results

They left with Tony's results and the neurologist's recommendation. "Tony Fishel is extremely intelligent and severely dyslexic. He requires at least 50% of his day in a program for dyslexic students."

Now, teachers who had said how well Tony read now said "I was just beginning to think Tony had some sort of problem."

Bob and Judy took copies of the neurologist's papers to the school superintendent. As predicted, he said he'd put Tony on the waiting list.

Bob told him that we understood it was illegal to put a child on a waiting list.

Finally, the superintendent said he'd need a week or two to make arrangements.

And sure enough, before long, Tony took the bus across town every day. He spent half the day in a small class with about seven other children. For the rest of the day, Tony was back in his usual class.

Tony

I remember going to Boston to see the neurologist but I don't remember much about the tests. Some of the tests were really easy for me. He told me to slow down and think about it but I kept going fast because I knew I could get them right.

The math problem was like being in school. I could do it mentally but couldn't do it on paper.

It was like reading. I couldn't do it like everyone else. I had to do it my way, starting with the answer and then trying to do it on paper

What I remember most was what the neurologist said at the end. He said I was very intelligent (I knew that) but that I might never read or write.

I didn't think about the word "might." I felt like it was hopeless and that I would never learn to read.

The special class was okay. I tried really hard to read their way but I still learned very little.

Parents: Talk to your child about dyslexia – about what it means – about famous and successful people who have dyslexia (check the Internet) – that having dyslexia does not mean you are stupid. It means you learn differently.

Students: Explain to people that you have dyslexia and you learn differently. When you have questions or problems, talk to your parents. Tell them if you are feeling upset or unhappy. Be sure to tell them if they can help you in any way. They love you and they really want to help.

Judy

I think the first three years of school, especially without a proper diagnosis, was the most painful time in Tony's life. Yes, knowing he might never read or write was hard but once you have a name for something, you can talk about it, explain why you can't read, and perhaps try new strategies.

Tony wasn't the only one who had begun to feel it was hopeless. When Tony started going to the new class with a teacher using the highly recommended Orton-Gillingham method I began feeling more hopeful.

We were lucky to live in a city that had a program for dyslexic students. Even today, it might be hard to find a program like that.

You are more likely to find a specialist who might work with a dyslexic student several times a week. You might be given a list of specialists in your area that you can hire to work with your child.

If the school doesn't recommend someone, you might try searching your computer for programs you can use at home. Whatever you do, don't give up. Your child needs your help.

Chapter 6.

Learning outside of class

fourth, fifth and sixth grades

In fourth, fifth and sixth grades, Tony spent half of each day with the dyslexia reading specialist. Meeting other dyslexic students might have helped him realize he wasn't the only person with this problem.

They were also good years in other ways.

Tony was in third grade when his parents bought a computer. The only thing they could do with it was play a simple game called Pong.

Their computer was the first one in the neighborhood. Kids came home from school with Tony just to see it. Showing other kids how to use the computer seemed to give Tony a little more self-confidence.

It was even better the next year when his
school bought the same kind of computer.
None of the teachers knew how to use it.
When a teacher had a question or problem,
they asked Tony to help them.

The teachers were afraid they'd break the
computer if they hit the wrong key. Tony
assured them that to break it, they'd need to
hit it with a hammer.

The teachers also went to Tony when the
computer stopped working as it often did.
Tony showed them how to turn the computer
off and then turn it on again. That always
solved the problem.

Explaining the computer to kids built his
self-image a little; showing teachers how
to use a computer built his self-image a lot
more. Every student in his class knew that
teachers came to get advice from Tony.

When Tony was in fourth grade, Judy was
working on a Master's degree in Biology.

For a class in entomology, she was required
to make an insect collection, all correctly

labeled. She started this project during the summer and had great helpers. She bought extra butterfly nets.

Tony often invited a friend. Judy set up a folding chair where she sat with her killing bottle, pins, and display boxes. The boys did nearly all the running and catching. They had fun and Judy had twice as many insects as were required for her class.

As they did this, Tony and his mother learned to identify the butterflies and sometimes she and Tony even recognized them from a moving car. Judy read books about research in the area and shared the most interesting stories with Tony. When he started fourth-grade Tony wanted to take the butterflies to show his teacher and the class. They first got the teacher's permission. The teacher probably wasn't expecting very much.

To her surprise, Tony showed up with several large display boxes filled with butterflies and other interesting insects Tony could identify all the butterflies and many of the others. He also shared some of the research stories he'd learned.

His teacher was really impressed. She got permission for Tony to take his display to every class in the school.

When Judy returned to her school, she learned that the entomology class had been cancelled because too few students had signed up.

She didn't care. She had learned everything she wanted to know, and she and Tony had a wonderful time.

Boy Scouts

That year Tony joined Cub Scouts. He enjoyed the Cub Scout activities. These boys were not in his classes so they didn't know that Tony couldn't read. By the time he reached sixth grade, he was a Boy Scout

Tony

One of the strongest memories of that year was going overnight camping with the Boy Scouts for the very first time. I was excited and nervous at the same time.

I had felt this same way going to sleep-overs with my friends. Many of those nights ended with me becoming too anxious. My mom or dad came to pick me up and take me home where I felt safe.

As we set up our single person tents, I felt only freedom and exhilaration. I had always wanted to go camping but our family never did that.

I felt safe enough being surrounded by not only the other scouts of my troop but 50 other troops at the Jamboree we were attending.

Then, my nightmares came. I was running from something but not sure what. It was dark. The ground was cold and wet. Branches seemed to reach out and claw at me. I turned back to see what was chasing me and saw only trees and their claws and darkness.

I tripped and felt the Earth and the leaves and dampness with such clarity that I realized I wasn't dreaming. I could taste blood on my fat lip, and I was breathing heavily. I stood up, looked for the monster, and saw a fire in the distance.

I looked down and saw that I was in my "tighty whities," sleep-walking alone in the woods in the middle of the night.

I was no longer on that island in the middle of the South Pacific Ocean, but I was still alone. That first, long ago dream, felt like a prophecy. The feelings of isolation and loneliness that I first felt in the Marshalls had not gone away.

Building Self-Confidence

While they couldn't help Tony learn to read, his parents tried very hard to make him feel better about himself and to help him succeed in other areas.

One summer, Tony decided to play Little League baseball. He wasn't very good at it and wasn't interested enough to practice.

In fifth and sixth grade, he played on a basketball team. While he was having fun, Tony didn't have the skills he needed and had no desire to spend hours throwing a basketball through a hoop.

For other children, sports might be an area where they could excel but it wasn't something Tony could do.

Parents and students: It's important for each child to have activities they love doing, something they are good at. If a child loves art or music, model planes, dancing or sports, parents should encourage them.

Students: help your parents understand what things you'd love to try doing. They won't know if you don't tell them.

Tony

It would have been nice if I had been good at sports but I wasn't. Playing baseball and basketball were things I wasn't good at and never would be.

In fifth and sixth grade, I played on a basketball team. I especially remember one of the boys on my basketball team. He was twice my size and seemed to have been playing for years.

He could throw the ball at the basket and it nearly always went in. He made more points in one game than all the rest of the team together.

Dungeons and Dragons

Tony's friend from church taught Tony to play Dungeons and Dragons. Tony's parents gradually bought him all the books.

Eventually, Tony wrote his own Dungeon and Dragons games. He dictated and his mother wrote them down. He then went on to teach other kids to play.

Tony

I enjoyed playing Dungeons and Dragons partly because it was something I really could do and I could do it well. I also hoped playing these games would help me learn to read.

When I was in school, I never felt like what I was trying to read was terribly important. For Dungeons and Dragons, I needed to learn all about the characters to play well.

No one was helping me by explaining the answer first. I understood the kind of information I needed and I learned how to find it.

Judy

As I watched Tony searching for the information about new characters, I wondered if it might help him learn to read. What was more important was that Tony seemed to be having a wonderful time.

Students: Notice that Tony spent several years trying different activities before he finally found something he liked. Learning to play Dungeons and Dragons wasn't easy. It took a lot of time and effort before he became a good player.

Tony also enjoyed building model airplanes. He showed them to one of his teachers who just happened to have models he never got around to building. He was happy to share some of them with

Tony joined the Military Miniature group. First, we saw a competition of their work. They took miniature metal figures of different characters and spent many long hours painting them and creating historical backgrounds.

Tony talked to several of the men and was invited to come to a meeting. Soon Tony was a member. The other members all seemed to be over 60 and all had figures they never used that they shared with Tony. Later, while they did military figures, Tony painted mostly fantasy figures.

Doing activities like this can help you feel good about yourself. It did for Tony.

Chapter 7.

Tony and the Apple

When Tony was in fifth grade, his mother was teaching seventh grade science. Tony often asked what she'd taught her students that day. One day Judy's lesson had an ant on the hat of a man on a moving train.

If the train is going 60 miles per hour north, and the man on the train is walking 4 miles per hour south, how fast is the man going? Then, if an ant on the man's hat is going 1 mile per hour north, how fast is the ant going?

Students were supposed to take the trains speed, 60 miles per hour north and subtract the man's speed in the opposite direction so the man was going 56 miles per hour north. In the question with the ant going 1 mile an hour north, the same direction the train was moving, the ant was going 57 miles per hour north.

Judy then explained that the book left out one important part. Speed questions should be "in relation to what?"

The man was actually walking 4 miles per hour south in relation to the train, but 56 miles per hour north in relation to the ground. Little did she know how fascinating this concept would be for Tony.

How Fast is an Apple?

Several weeks later, Judy returned from work to find Tony sitting at the kitchen table, staring at an apple. "Mom," he said, "How fast is an apple?"

"That apple on the table?" she asked. "It doesn't look to me like it's moving at all."

"Come on, Mom. Think about it," Tony insisted. "How fast is it moving?" She pondered this problem for several minutes and finally said, "I guess the apple is going as fast as the earth is going."

"Good," he said. "Now we need to think about how fast the earth is moving. But the earth is moving in different ways.

"It's moving around its own axis. It's moving around the sun. The sun is moving in relation to the solar system and the solar system is moving around the galaxy and probably even more ways."

They got out an encyclopedia and started with the easiest way of moving. The earth is close to 25,000 miles around at the equator.

The earth turns around once on its axis in one day. Therefore, the apple is moving approximately 25, 000 miles a day at the equator. With 24 hours in a day, we can divide 25,000 by 24. This means it is moving roughly 1,000 miles per hour.

Over the next several months, Tony added to his explanations of the Apple's movement. The first were two fairly obvious observations.

First, the distance around the earth is greatest at the equator and very tiny at the poles. This means the measurement of the apple's speed would need to include the distance from the equator.

His second observation was that climbing a mountain, was like making your circumference larger. If you dug a deep hole and went down into the earth, your circumference would be less. To calculate the speed of the apple, we need to know the apple's distance from the equator and its distance above or below sea level.

The observation that was most surprising was when Tony came home from school one day all excited and asked, "Guess what Mom? Did you know that the apple moves faster at night than it does during the day?"

Judy couldn't figure this one out. She did wonder what he should have been doing in school when he was thinking about the apple.

"At night," Tony explained, "the place where you are on earth is going the same direction as the movement of the earth around the sun.

You can put the two speeds together so the earth is going faster.

During the day, the movement of the earth's rotation is opposite to the movement of the earth around the sun. With the combined movements, the earth is going more slowly in relation to the sun. This means that to calculate the speed of the apple, we need to know what time it is." If you don't understand this, don't worry. It really is confusing.

The last insight about the speed of his apple came when Tony was in high school. "Did you know," he asked his mother when he got home from school, "that the speed of the apple depends on the day of the year?"

Again, his mother had no clue.

"You know how the earth goes around the sun? It doesn't move in a circle; it's an elliptical orbit." She nodded.

"When the earth is closer to the sun it goes faster because of the sun's gravity. When it's farther away from the sun, the earth moves more slowly. So, if you want a formula for the speed of the apple, it would need to include the day of the year."

Tony

Thinking about the apple was exciting. I was asking a question I'd never heard asked and it pushed me to think creatively as well as using my knowledge about the solar system to answer it by myself.

That was exciting and it was something I really could do well. Talking to my parents about it was also fun because I could understand something they hadn't ever thought about.

Judy

Thinking about the movement of the apple was fun. I enjoyed listening to his amazing discoveries. It was obvious that Tony was extremely intelligent. He often asked wonderful questions but this was his most memorable question.

College Academy

Tony's friend, David, had gone to a summer program the summer before. College Academy was a program for gifted kids in grades 4-8. Tony decided he wanted to go. Judy called to ask if her son who was very bright but dyslexic could attend their program.

They said certainly, he could. He would not need to read in these classes.

Just being accepted in a program for gifted students seemed to improve Tony's self- confidence and he had a wonderful time. He took classes like Dungeons and Dragons, rocketry, and a class in small engine repair.

In the Small Engine Repair class, students learned to take apart and put together lawn mower engines. Tony managed to take them apart and put them together twice while other students did it once.

His teacher was so delighted with his skills that he built a little trophy and gave it to Tony at the end of the program. Tony returned to College Academy every year through eighth grade.

Tony

I loved College Academy. It wasn't like school. No one cared if I could read. I was good at doing the various activities and enjoyed being in classes with other smart kids. I really fit in. I wished school was like this.

Judy

Did the Special Class Help?

Now, at the end of sixth grade, we had the all-important question. After 3½ years in the special reading program for children with dyslexia, did Tony learn to read?

By this time, we had learned to check Tony's improvement for ourselves. His teacher said Tony was now reading at a second-grade level.

Tony seemed to read fairly well from the second-grade book they used in his class. However, with another second-grade book, Tony was lost.

We tried a first-grade book. He couldn't read that either. Tony thought he was reading, not faking it, but neither Tony nor his teacher realized it was still mostly memory and guessing.

Tony

My mother just asked me if I remember working hard in the special class or if I had given up trying. I think it was both. I tried really hard in the beginning but, when nothing helped, I just gave up.

My mother asked another question. She wanted to know how I felt about myself in elementary school – if I thought I was stupid or if I felt good about myself.

To begin with, I always knew I was really smart. It wasn't just the neurologist telling me this. My parents told me this many, many times. But it didn't make sense. If I was so smart, why couldn't I learn to read?

I also remember thinking, "Why me? Why can't I fit in? Why can't I read?

Parents: Notice that in spite of his problems, Tony firmly believed that he was really smart. This is very important. Children who believe they are dumb have no reason to keep trying. Tell them over and over how smart they are.

Judy

Tony seemed to have learned the letters of the alphabet and most of the letter sounds but he still could not read and he could not write well enough for anyone to read.

This was discouraging. If the best trained teacher in Brockton couldn't teach him to read, how would he ever learn?

This meant Tony would begin middle school, still completely unable to read or write.

Chapter 8.

Middle School: A Whole New World

Soon after Tony finished sixth grade, his family moved to Rhode Island. While looking for a house, they asked which schools had the best programs for dyslexic students. Two school systems were recommended. They chose Barrington. This opened up a whole new world for Tony.

Judy asked Tony if he thought it would be best to repeat sixth grade or to go straight to Middle School. After some discussion, he chose Middle School.

Now they realize that another year of elementary school would have been a terrible choice. He would have been even more depressed. In Middle School, reading was less of an issue. In Middle School, he could really be a success.

They moved to Rhode Island early in the summer and read in the newspaper that they had a Pop Warner Football Team for students his age. He had never been a football fan but decided he'd like to try it, mainly to begin meeting some of the boys in his school. Tony looked great in his uniform but spent most of the games sitting on the bench.

Middle School

In the Middle School, Tony was placed in all regular classes but he also had a special education teacher, Mrs. Levesque, who helped him when needed.

All of his teachers knew Tony was dyslexic; they knew he couldn't read or write. When he had a test or work sheet, he'd leave class with the test and hurry down the hall to the special ed room.

Mrs. Levesque stopped what she was doing and read the questions. Tony told her the answers and she would write them down. He took his paper back to the class before most of the students had finished.

Tony

Middle school was a happy time. At first it was hard to adjust to being in a new house, a new neighborhood, and a new school where I didn't know anyone. I missed my old friends.

The best thing was that with help from Mrs. Levesque and my mother, I could do well in all my classes.

Boy Scouts

Once school started, Tony joined a Boy Scout troop. Troop 2 had a great reputation in town. They were the boys who all intended to work hard and become Eagle Scouts.

At Boy Scout camp, they were the boys who were up early, marched a mile and then jumped into the cold lake before any of the other troops were awake,

In the Memorial Day parades, the other scout troops walked; these scouts marched. In fact, they marched quickstep.

In spite of his inability to read, Tony earned badge after badge, and he did reach the goal of Eagle Scout.

Tony was proud to be in Troop 2. They went camping, sleeping in tents even in the coldest part of the winter. Like the other boys, he wanted to show that he could do things that were hard.

Tony

I loved being in Boy Scouts. My inability to read was not a problem there. The discipline in our troop was tough but it was tough for all of us.

Finally, Tony is a good student

Tony came home after school and his mother helped him with his homework. She never did homework for him. Like his special ed teacher, she would read the lesson or his worksheets, Tony would tell her the answers, and she'd write them down.

At the end of the first grading period,

Tony's parents were surprised to read that he needed to do his homework. Judy knew she and Tony had done all the work. Why weren't the teachers getting it?

There was a simple answer. The homework was lost in Tony's backpack. When the teachers asked for homework, Tony felt around in his backpack, but if he couldn't find it, he forgot about it. They began using a homework folder. The pocket on one side was for homework he needed to do. The pocket on the other side was for completed homework.

Judy had read that it was best for parents not to try teaching their child because they so often would end up nagging the child to do their homework.

The Fishels' solution was to put Tony in charge. When he came home from school, his mother would ask these questions.

First, what do you have for homework?

Second, how long will it take to finish?

Third, how long will you want my help?

Fourth, will you start now or after dinner?

Finally, let me know when you need help.

Tony

I missed my old friends. But now, with the help from Mrs. Levesque and my mother, I did well in all my classes. Best of all I had several friends who were in my classes and two friends in my neighborhood. I was still shy and not good at making friends but I felt like I fit in.

Sure, I had some problems. There were a few bullies in my neighborhood. I had never dealt with bullies before, but there was a tough kid in the neighborhood who threatened to beat up a smaller and younger boy. I had never been in a fight before but I defended the younger kid and won.

The bully hurried home to complain to his father who happened to be a policeman. His dad called my father, threatening to take us to court and sue us if I beat up his son again. I had already told my father what happened. The bully's dad yelled that he would wear his police uniform to court. Everyone would believe him.

My father calmly responded, "Please go ahead and wear your uniform and I will wear mine, my clerical robes."

Yes, my Dad was a preacher. Then, he nonchalantly hung up the phone.

Seeing my father stand up for me like that was, and still is, one of my best memories. I sometimes take for granted how hard and how much my mother, my father, and my sister supported me and stood up and fought for me.

There was also a bully in the Middle School who tripped students going up or down stairs. I got mad one day when he tripped someone and I and punched him.

Both of us were suspended for fighting. The principal told my parents not to punish me. He said they should be proud of me. The other kid was a trouble maker. Many students complained but the teachers never caught him tripping kids. The principal said it was about time someone did something about it.

Judy

Tony started seventh grade without being able to read or write but his self-confidence was beginning to improve.

In elementary school, he used to walk around hunched over, not saying much, as if he wanted to be invisible.

Now he was standing tall, smiling, and making friends in his classes for the first time.

Parents and Students Tony had problems finding his homework in his book bag. Students with dyslexia commonly need help getting organized. Try using a homework folder.

You should also notice how Bob and Judy helped Tony organize his time. They did not tell him what to do and when to do it. They asked questions that helped him plan his own time.

You should also be aware that we spent a great deal of time and effort to improve Tony's self-confidence. A student who expects to fail probably will fail. When you feel good about yourself, you are usually more successful.

Chapter 9.

Four Life-changing Events

First Event: Tony Goes to Yale

The most astonishing event in seventh grade was Tony's trip to Yale where his sister was a student. Thamora gave Tony a Yale sweatshirt for Christmas. Later she invited him to spend a weekend with her to see what it was like in college.

To get there, he would have to take the train. Tony had never even been on a train. He would need to recognize his stop, so his parents wrote "New Haven" on an index card. He assured us he would recognize it when he heard it announced or if he saw a sign.

When he got home, he told his parents what happened on his trip to New Haven.

Tony

I was wearing my Yale Sweatshirt on the train. Someone asked if I was a Yale Student. I told them, **"Yes. I'm doing graduate work at Yale."**

The people who were listening said "You look awfully young to be a graduate student." "I know," I said. "**I started college when I was twelve.**" (Actually, I was twelve then but I'd just heard about students starting college when they were twelve)

"What are you studying?" they asked. **"I'm doing research in Particle Physics,"** I told them. I explained Particle Physics and described my research.

My parents first question was

"Tony, HOW did you do that?"

I said "You remember. It was on a Nova program a couple months ago." They vaguely remembered the program but had forgotten all the details. Maybe they didn't find it as exciting as I did.

"Did they believe you?" Dad asked. "I don't know," I said. "Maybe not at the beginning, but by at the end they might have."

Judy

Tony didn't always have an amazing memory. He could forget his homework assignments. He could forget people's names. He could forget to tell us about a phone call that we should return. But when it was related to science, his memory was amazing.

Tony

I hadn't planned to do this and I didn't really expect them to believe me but when they asked if I was a Yale Student, I thought it would be fun to say I was.

Then, when I started, I kept going, telling them the most outrageous things that came to mind. They probably learned something about particle physics. That part was true.

I had great fun on the train but never tried to do that again. The best part was shocking my parents when I got home. Being at Yale was also great. I met a lot of Thamora's friends and started to think about going to college.

Special Events: Science Fairs

Each year the Middle School had a Science Fair. Participation was optional. In seventh grade, Tony compared the effects of acid rain on Narragansett Bay (salt water) and the Palmer River (mostly fresh water.

Tony's project won an award at his school and he went on to the State Science Fair. At the state fair, he won a second-place ribbon in his category.

More important was the opportunity to check out all the other projects and to see what kind of projects won the big awards. Tony began thinking about what he might do the next year to get a first-place ribbon.

In eighth grade, Tony was eager to do a Science Fair project that was better than before. He and his mother did some serious brainstorming and decided to use planaria.

If you cut these small flatworms in half, each half forms a complete flatworm. You could slice the head and grow a flatworm with two or more heads.

Tony's research question was "Do planaria regenerate differently in water mixed with different substances?" He decided to add a little salt, vinegar, ammonia and other substances to the water.

To his dismay, on his first efforts, the planaria all died. They ordered more planaria and tried again They all died again.

This time Tony made an interesting discovery. Some of the planaria died by curling up tightly; others died in a relaxed position. This became his new question. "Why do planaria die one way in some chemicals and die differently in others?"

Tony took a first-place ribbon in his category and won special awards for projects related to medicine, and for the best use of pictures.

Judy still enjoys calling his project "How many ways can an eighth-grade boy kill planaria?"

Tony

Science Fair projects were fun but they were a lot of work. I knew I could do them well and, if I was going to teach physics, I would need some experience doing experiments.

I also liked thinking about good questions and trying to discover the answers. Again, I could not have done it without my mom's help.

Judy

I tried hard to let Tony do the hard work and was sometimes surprised at his conclusions. When we did library research, I still had to find the most important information and read it to Tony.

When we did the displays for the Science Fairs, we planned the layout together but I did all the writing. You couldn't read his writing.

Tony was on his own, of course, when it came to explaining his work to the judges. He had no problem with this. This was one more activity that helped Tony feel good about himself.

Third Event: Teaching School

The next event occurred when Tony was in seventh grade, his first year in Rhode Island. Tony's school had a teacher workshop day. The school where Judy was teaching was in the next county and had school as usual.

Tony announced that he was planning to go to school with his mother and she thought it was a great idea.

Tony's next announcement was that he would teach her classes. Notice that he didn't ask if he could do this. He knew she'd agree.

Judy expected him to teach something related to science, that he might tell them about his apple. "No," Tony said firmly. "I will teach them about dyslexia."

Judy was teaching seventh grade science so Tony would be teaching students his own age. She couldn't imagine what he could tell her students that would fill the one-hour classes, but decided she could fill in if necessary. She did suggest that Tony work on his lesson plan.

At the beginning of each class, Judy introduced Tony and let him explain what he was going to tell them.

He began by telling them he was dyslexic and that they could all read and write better than he could but that being dyslexic

or having other learning differences did
not mean that you were stupid. You could
be dyslexic and still be very intelligent.
His main lesson was that people learn
differently.

It also meant they needed to work harder.

He told them he planned to go to college.
It wouldn't be easy but, if he worked very
hard, he could do it.

The response was amazing. These students
hurried out to find brothers, sisters, or
friends with learning problems, telling them
about Tony and urging them to get one
of their teachers to give them permission
to hear Tony.

Each period of the day, we had students
appear with notes from their teachers.

Every seat was soon filled and students stood
or sat around the sides of the classroom. The
number of students increased as the day
went on. Some even came to hear him again.

Judy

Tony's talk was an immense success. We decided Tony would come teach my classes one day every year and we soon began inviting special education teachers to bring their students.

These experiences had to have built up his self-image and self-confidence. This early teaching experience also helped him later as a teacher.

Tony

I wasn't sure I could do this, but I felt good at the front of the class telling them about dyslexia. I know some people don't like public speaking, but it was easy for me.

My mother had talked to me about her classes and she made it clear that I was not the only one struggling to learn, be it reading, math or science.

I did not feel so different from her students. I know lots of kids found school to be a struggle. It wasn't just me.

Somehow, I felt like I could explain that they might have learning problems like I did, that they were not alone, and that they could still be a success if they worked hard.

I was surprised to see so many kids who were not in my mother's class come to hear me that first time.

I don't know if they came to learn about dyslexia or because they wanted to see a seventh grader teaching a class. Either way, it made me feel really good and I looked forward to doing this every year.

Judy

I was amazed at Tony's success. When I was teaching in the high school, he spoke to my high school class. When I was teaching physics, he spoke to them. Every time he spoke, we had students I didn't know who came to hear Tony.

My students told their parents and their brothers and sisters. Each year my new students would ask, "When is Tony coming? I will never forget meeting Billy's mother. She did not say, "You are Billy's Science teacher."

She said "You are Tony's mother. Billy is still talking about Tony. He says that if Tony can go to college, he could do that too."

Tony only stopped coming when he was teaching his own classes. These experiences had to have built up his confidence and made he feel good about himself. This early teaching experience also helped him later as a teacher.

Fourth Event: Books on Tape

The next life changing event, came when Mrs. Levesque, Tony's special ed teacher, told his parents that Tony would be eligible to get *Books on Tape* from the Library for the Blind – later called the Library for the Blind and Dyslexic.

He could get all of his textbooks on tape and also get any other book he wanted to read. If it wasn't already on tape, they would have someone tape it for him. The Fishels couldn't imagine why no one told them earlier.

Tony tried using taped textbooks but decided he preferred having his mother read the textbooks. He liked it when she paused to see if he understood something or when she related the new information to something he'd already learned. He also liked to ask questions as she read to him.

Being able to read any book he wanted was amazing. His Dungeons and Dragons teacher at College Academy had told him he'd like reading *The Lord of the Rings* and *The Hobbit* by Tolkien.

The first book on tape he ordered was *The Lord of the Rings.* Then, Tony wanted a copy of the book. He didn't want a library book; he wanted to own the book.

HOW TONY TAUGHT HIMSELF TO READ

Every afternoon after school Tony put on his headphones, turned on the tape player, and sat with his book in his hand ready to listen to *The Lord of the Rings.* No one told him to follow along with his book, but what a difference it made! When he finished the book, he started over again, still following along as he read. He read *The Lord of the Rings* again and again. He read the book four or five times. Eventually, he was reading aloud along with the tape.

I suspect he had pretty much memorized the book and finally, he was able to read the book without the tape.

Then, he began reading the Hobbit. Again, he read it at least four times. Tony did not do this so he would learn to read. Even when he finished, he didn't realize that he had learned to read. He assumed that he had just memorized the words.

Even his parents had no idea he was learning to read. Like Tony, they thought he was just memorizing the words.

They should have understood that **memorizing the words is really another way of learning to read.** Tony later realized this was called the whole language approach.

They were all surprised, when the 'end of the year' test scores at school were released. Tony was now reading at a third-grade level.

Tony had done what the reading teachers couldn't do but he didn't know that he had done it.

He taught himself to read.

Tony

As far as I can remember, no one suggested that I follow along in the book while listening to the tapes. I don't think I really expected I could learn to read this way but, somehow, I thought it would be important to follow in the book.

I remember that I really wanted to read that book. It wasn't just something I had to read for class.

I really wanted to know what was inside that book and it made sense that seeing the words along with hearing the words would help me understand the book.

When I went to bed, I would often be worried about monsters and things coming to get me. Before we moved to Barrington I would more than occasionally try to sneak into my parents' bed or at least their bed room to fall asleep.

During one of those nights, before my father sent me back to my room, I heard something amazing. Someone was reading "The Return of the King" on the radio. I loved it when my parents or teachers read to me.

I found the stories in books fascinating but inaccessible unless they were read to me.

I was really excited to get books on
tape. I don't think I really expected
I could learn to read this way, but
I really wanted to know the rest of
the story. I wanted to know what was
inside that book.

It made sense. Seeing words along with
hearing them would help me remember
what the words looked like. Sounding
words out never seemed to work.
Remembering words and what they
sounded like usually worked faster and
eventually became my default instead of
the phonics approach.

I knew that many people with dyslexia
learn best using phonics like with the
Orton-Gillingham program.

For some reason, I seemed to learn
best with the whole language approach,
memorizing the words instead of
sounding them out.

While it was exciting to be able to read,
reading at a third-grade level wasn't
good enough for reading books in school

I still needed help from Mrs. Levesque and, at home, I needed my mother to help with my homework.

But I went from not being able to read to reading at a third- grade level. I felt there was hope for me.

Could other students learn this way? I don't think it would work if the student was only half-way interested. I was totally concentrating as I read, trying to absorb every word.

Judy

I would suggest starting with easier books. The Lord of the Rings is hard. If Tony could do it you might also teach yourself to read.

Tony read a few fairly simple books but he didn't read them more than once. Perhaps he hadn't found another book that he was so determined to read. Tony was still reading at a third-grade level in high school, in college, and when he finished graduate school.

Chapter 10.

High School is Different

Grades 9 and 10

Tony talked to each of his teachers at the beginning of school. He explained that he was dyslexic and that his IEP (Individual Educational Plan) required help with reading and writing.

His Spanish teacher put tests on a tape. Tony used two tape recorders, one to listen to questions and one to record his answers. When a classmate complained that Tony didn't lose points for spelling errors, the teacher said, "That's true, and you don't lose points for poor pronunciation."

In high school, note-taking is important. Tony tried taking notes but he couldn't read what he had written and neither could his mother.

Tony asked for permission to tape record his classes. Only his biology teacher objected. Tony recorded her anyway, keeping his tape recorder in his backpack. It worked well enough until the day he reached into his backpack and hit play instead of record. Everyone heard the teacher's voice but she wasn't speaking.

After that, Tony found several girls who took good notes and asked them to make copies for him. His mother read their notes and they decided which information he might be tested on. Tony used notes on index cards to prepare for tests. In other classes, he decided he didn't need notes. He could listen carefully and remember.

The high school special education program was not like the program in the middle school. Tony wasn't even sure the teachers knew who he was. Instead of offering help with tests, they focused on helping kids with their homework. Tony preferred the help he got at home. He decided this was a waste of his time so he signed himself out of the program and then told his parents. His parents agreed. This was his decision to make.

He made another wise decision. He had joined the wrestling team. They practiced several hours every day and Tony came home feeling too tired to do homework.

He discovered that none of his teammates were taking classes as difficult as his. They didn't need time for homework.

He explained to the coach that he needed time to keep up with his schoolwork and he dropped the team. His parents were surprised but proud of Tony's decision.

One of Tony's goals was to make passing grades just like other students WITHOUT needing extra help but that still wasn't realistic. His mother remembers the first time he tried reading one of his textbooks. He was in tenth grade. He came home one afternoon and announced that he had already read his chemistry assignment.

Most students would think the chemistry book was the hardest to read. Tony said that because it was hard, their assignments were very short. Then in most books, small words looked like other small words. "In chemistry," he said, "Big words don't look like other words."

His mother thinks it helped that Tony was familiar with the vocabulary in science. He had a better chance than most students of guessing what the big words were.

The Physics of Toys

Judy needed to take additional classes to update her teaching certificate. One class was 'The Physics of Toys." After the first class, she asked the professor if she could bring her son with her, explaining that he was a future physics teacher. Tony went with her week after week for the whole semester and he loved it. He understood some of the concepts faster than she did.

Critical Thinking

Later that year, Judy was planning to attend a weekend workshop on Critical Thinking. Tony was eager to go with her and he fit in well. Tony and Judy worked in different small groups and Judy was only a little surprised to find that Tony was chosen to make the reports for his group.

Tony gets his boat

When Tony was in ninth grade, his family visited grandparents in Florida. His grandfather showed Tony how to run his boat, a Boston Whaler with an outboard engine.

That summer, Tony's grandfather died. Their family went back to Florida for Christmas and a memorial service.

Thamora was given grandpa's car since their grandmother had a car of her own. Tony was given the boat since he was the only person in the family who knew how to use it. With the car pulling the boat, they drove back to Rhode Island.

That summer, Tony decided to get rich selling quahogs, the local clams. He bought a clam rake for about $100 and started to work. Somehow, every time he earned money, he needed a new propeller, he needed gas, or he lost his rake and needed a new one. He lost money faster than he earned it.

Over the next several summers, Tony used the boat to have fun with his friends. They had a giant inner tube that was especially exciting when Tony pulled the tube and a friend behind the boat.

Tony

Barrington was one of those towns with many really rich people. Just driving through town, you could see many elegant homes. At school I felt like I didn't fit in because we weren't rich.

When I got the boat, all that changed. I had a boat and none of my friends had one. I could take them on the boat or pull them on that inner tube. It was almost like being rich. Now, finally, I really felt like I fit in.

Tony as College Academy Teacher

When it was time to sign up for College Academy, Tony, now too old to attend, asked if he could teach. The usual rule was that high school students could be assistants, running errands for the staff.

College students could teach the non-academic classes like Rocketry or Dungeons and Dragons, but only certified teachers could teach academic classes like Fun with Physics and Math Madness.

Tony, now well known by the staff, asked if he could please teach that summer. He taught Rocketry and Dungeons and Dragons and he was a hit with the students.

By the end of the summer, parents were asking what Tony would be teaching the next summer because their children wanted to sign up for whatever he was teaching. This meant the staff needed to find other classes Tony could teach.

When Tony started college and had an ever-growing fan club, they let him teach Fun with Physics and Math Madness.

Judy gave him her teaching materials.

Tony used many activities his mother had used but added others of his own.

Tony

Teaching at College Academy was great fun and I even got paid for having a good time. I worked hard to make my classes interesting. All my years as a student at College Academy made that pretty easy.

Judy

Tony and I were the only mother and son teaching at College Academy at the same time. I remember thinking that this opportunity to teach would give Tony experience that would help him prepared to be a teacher someday.

I also thought it might even help him get a teaching job. After all, most students straight out of college don't have any teaching experience.

Back to the Philippines

Bob was invited to lead a college work project in the Philippines while Tony was in tenth grade. He said it would be nice for Tony to go along but being away from school for a month was out of the question.

By now, Tony was an expert in self advocating. He went to each of his teachers and got their permission.

In gym, he agreed to make up every class he would miss with early make-up gym classes. For art, he would stay after school to complete all of his ceramic projects. For Algebra II, he would take his book with him and complete all the assignments he missed. For Chemistry, the teacher pretty much just said, "Have a good Time."

Tony knew it would be hard to convince his parents to let him go but, with all of his teachers agreeing, how could they say no? He went and had a wonderful time.

Science Fair - Kaleidoscopes

When Tony was in tenth grade, his Science Fair project was the best yet. He studied kaleidoscopes. They found a shop that cut mirrors into the shapes he wanted

He built kaleidoscopes with two mirrors, three mirrors and four mirrors. The four-mirror kaleidoscope had a large opening at one end and smaller opening at the other.

Again, Tony won a first place at the State Science Fair, along with an award for math (he compared the angles of the mirrors to the number of reflections you could see). And, of course, he again won an award for the use of photography.

Judy

As usual, Tony had no problem talking to the judges and answering their questions. Many people were interested in kaleidoscopes so Tony was busy all day explaining what he had learned.

Tony

Later, we created Kaleidoscopes using full-length mirrors. With two mirrors, you see a single row of images. With three mirrors, images spread out in all directions.

Later, we used our "Human Kaleidoscopes" in College Academy and other classes.

We even used them to make a presentation at the National Science

Teacher Association Conference in Boston. We had slides taken through kaleidoscopes.

Mom ran the projector and let me explain what they were seeing. We also had a "Human Kaleidoscope" set up so they could look through it for themselves.

Thinking About College

Tenth grade was also the year Tony and his parents decided it was time for Tony's college tours. While on this trip, someone mentioned that Landmark College had a program just for dyslexic students. That seemed like a good choice for Tony.

They also learned there was a Landmark High School. They had a full high school program except for AP classes. The classes were small and, for reading, the teachers taught one student at a time.

Judy

Landmark is a residential school. Tony occasionally came home for weekends taking the train to Boston, the subway to the bus station and the bus to Providence where we picked him up.

Tony's reading hadn't improved in Barrington. We hoped he would improve his skills at Landmark.

Tony

I already knew that I wanted to be a high school physics teacher. I would take physics my junior year and AP Physics when I was a senior.

They had a physics class at Landmark and promised I could take it. Landmark seemed like a good school.

Chapter 11.

Grades 11 and 12

Junior Year at Landmark

Landmark is northeast of Boston and it cost more than any of the colleges we considered. But, with all the individual attention they offered, it seemed to be worth the cost. Tony applied and was accepted.

Judy

On the day when students arrived, parents were invited to visit the classrooms and learn more about their programs.

I have two memories of that day. First, I visited the science classroom where one of the students had a large boa constrictor draped around his shoulder. "Do you want to touch him?" he asked.

I touched it. Tony just smiled. He knew his mother wasn't scared of snakes.

The boy took the snake off of his shoulder. "Want to hold him?" he asked, holding the snake out, sure she would back away.

"Of course," I said, taking the snake and putting it over my shoulders, While the boys were disappointed, Tony was proud of his me.

I also remember a speaker explaining how important it was for their students to self-advocate, to tell teachers about their problems and to ask for help when they needed it. Tony was already self-advocating in high school but it seemed great to reinforce what he was already doing.

Bob

I went to a different event. The speaker talked about the way most children with dyslexia have low self-images. Some gave up easily and others were class clowns or they got into trouble in school.

Tony never acted like a class clown or got into trouble. He was polite, well- behaved and got along well with his teachers.

After the talk, I told the speaker about Tony who seemed to be the opposite and I told him about Tony's adventure on his train ride to Yale. The speaker laughed and said there was a name for this: grandiosity.

People with grandiosity sometimes think they can fly a plane without taking lessons or they do operations without going to medical school.

Grandiosity might have fit Tony if he tried things like that regularly, but he didn't. Tony seemed to be a well-balanced student who lacked skills in reading and writing.

Finally, Bob and Judy said goodbye to Tony and headed home.

Tony's First Days at Landmark

Tony spent most of the first several days, walking up to other students and introducing himself, asking where they were from, trying for the first time in his life to make friends.

As a result, Tony was elected president of his dorm. One student told Bob and Judy later that Tony was obviously a shy kid pretending to be popular. For Tony, pretending to be outgoing and popular seemed to have worked.

The next day, the students were tested and the day after that, they received their schedules. Tony was scheduled for marine biology instead of physics.

He went to his teacher and explained that someone made a mistake. He was supposed to take physics. The teacher explained that he couldn't take physics because he needed to read at fourth grade level to take physics.

They had no idea that Tony was experienced in self-advocating. After talking to his teacher, he went to the department head, and got the same answer. He went to the next level and got the same answer. He finally went to the head of the school and still, he got the same answer.

Tony finally called his parents and they spoke to the head of the school. They began by explaining that Tony had been promised that he could take physics and that he would never have gone to Landmark if he couldn't take physics.

They also pointed out that the people at Landmark were teaching students to self-advocate. Well, Tony was self-advocating like crazy and he was still being ignored. Now they were advocating for him.

The principal pointed out that students without a fourth-grade reading level were likely to fail physics.

"That's fine," Judy said. "We don't care if he fails. We just want him in that class."

Finally, two weeks after classes started, Tony was finally placed in the physics class. His parents suspect that the teacher had been told that Tony wasn't expected to do very well.

The next event is really hard to believe. And no, Tony's parents never talked to the teacher.

Tony's First Day in Physics

On Tony's first day in the physics class, the teacher pointed at a large rock on his desk. He asked the students "How fast is this rock going?" You can imagine what happened next.

After several students pointed out that the rock wasn't going anywhere, Tony raised his hand. He pointed out that, in relation to the desk or even the ground, the rock wasn't moving, but that it moved in many ways in relation to the sun or other objects in the universe.

He then spent most of the period sharing with them the many ways the rock, along with the earth, was moving. It is likely the teacher learned things he hadn't known and he probably also realized that this student wasn't going to have any problems in his class.

At the end of the first half of the year, Tony and one other student were honored for the best work in physics. Then, there was a program for Massachusetts students taking physics. Top students were invited to participate in a physics class at Harvard.

The class was "Waves, Particles, and the Structure of Matter." The physics teacher drove Tony and the other top student every week to their class at Harvard.

Tony was thrilled. This part of his Landmark experience was fantastic. His other classes were just okay. His reading class was a waste of time.

Tony was allowed to choose the book he wanted to read. He chose *A Brief History of Time* by Stephen Hawking. His teacher said she wouldn't understand that book.

"No problem," Tony assured her, "You help me read it and I'll explain what it means." While he enjoyed reading the book, his reading level did not improve.

Tony Takes the SAT

The other important event that year was that the juniors took the SAT. They had their choice of having someone read the questions for them, of having the questions on tape, or taking them the usual way but with unlimited time.

If he'd asked his mother's opinion, she would have urged Tony to take the first option. She had watched Tony do a practice test. He had struggled with one question and finally asked her a question.

"Mom, what is a kizel? I can't answer the question unless I know what a kizel is." Judy had no idea what a kizel was either until she looked at the test. The word was chisel. It was an analogy question like a chisel is to wood as a knife is to a fork, plate or cake.

Tony was trying to sound out the word. In the word, chemistry, ch sounds like a K so it seemed reasonable that ch in chisel would also sound like k.

Tony set out bravely to face the SAT. When he got stuck, he just kept trying to figure it out. While the test normally takes 3 hours, Tony worked all morning, took a lunch break and then worked until dinner time.

He still wasn't finished so he continued working most of the next day. He said there were some students who took much longer than he did.

To their surprise, Tony's scores were acceptable for most of the colleges they had considered, even a little above average.

Judy

The year at Landmark was a good year for Tony, especially with his great success in physics. It certainly helped him see how important it was to self-advocate.

Now I suspect the reason Tony's reading didn't improve as we had hoped was because when Tony didn't recognize a word, his teacher probably told him what it was. I think Tony would have learned more without her help.

Tony

Going to Landmark was great. I was frustrated at first when they wouldn't let me take physics. Thank goodness, we finally convinced them.

I loved that class because it finally gave me an opportunity to show them what I already knew plus it was easy to learn more.

Going to that class at Harvard was amazing. We even got to go in the labs where they were doing experiments to see if cold fusion was real.

Going to a new school also made it possible for me to try a new personality. I wanted people to see me as popular, self-confident, and friendly. I wanted people to see me not as a dork or someone who didn't fit in. It worked a lot better than I had expected.

Senior Year Back at Home

The next year, Tony was back in Rhode Island, back in a school where he could take AP Physics. When Tony started his senior year, he not only took AP Physics, he also took AP English.

His parents would never have suggested AP English but Tony had talked to the teacher first and gotten his permission before telling his parents

He explained that going back over all the boring grammar would be harder for him. He thought discussing literature would be more exciting and even easier for him.

One surprise was that many students who hadn't known Tony well before didn't recognize him now. They thought he was a new student.

He was now so confident and outgoing that he seemed to be a different person. Girls who had ignored him before now found him interesting. Later in the year, Tony even played the lead role in a play, something he would never have tried before.

For Tony's high school graduation, he used flowers from our garden to decorate his graduation cap. When he got to the high school, they made he take off the flowers, but they didn't notice when he put the flowers back under his robe.

Once out on the football field where the graduates were seated, he calmly took out his flowers and put them back on his cap.

What we really loved was that one of his teachers who admired the flowers earlier told Tony she was really glad when he put the flowers back on his cap. Tony had many wonderful teachers.

Chapter 12.

Tony Starts College

Tony, still reading at third-grade level, was accepted at Boston University. They had a two-year program for students with learning disabilities.

Tony

During the first two years of BU, I was in a program called College of Basic Studies, or CBS. Sometimes it was referred to as "Cute but Stupid" or "College of Beer and Sleep."

In the second semester of the second year, we took 2 classes at CBS and two regular BU classes. If we passed, we could transfer to any other college at BU.

Everything went pretty well at first.

My years in college were both wonderful and excruciating. I'm not sure if I partied so much because college was difficult or if college was difficult because I partied so much.

Note-taking

In most of my classes, taking notes was more of a distraction than a tool to help me study.

My handwriting was so bad and my spelling so illegible, that I could not decipher my notes when I got home.

I spent so much brain power taking illegible notes that I did not remember the class or lecture. In most classes I didn't take any notes.

I doodled as I listened very carefully to what the teacher said. I might write down a sentence or two every now and then but nothing to study.

In all my classes on the first day I would talk to the professor after class about me being dyslexic and how taking notes did not work.

I told them not to worry if I sat in the front row just staring at them or doodling. I also asked if they could give me the notes or have another student copy theirs for me. This always seemed to impress my professors.

Fear of Failure

When I tried to study, it started to overwhelm me and I went to clubs or raves to escape the fear of failure. Looking back on them, it was also those years that depression really started to affect my life.

I'm sure it started in high school but in college it became a weekly ritual. Every Sunday night was a time of worrying, fear, isolation and crippling self-doubt.

By Wednesday I would realize things weren't as bad as they seemed or that things were so terrible that, in either case, partying to rave music was a good solution.

I would forget about school and focus on being a DJ and from Thursday to Sunday afternoon I had some of the best times of my life.

Then, as the sun went down on the weekend, so would my spirts and, before long, I would find myself in that place again.

Judy

I remember Tony talking about becoming a DJ. He spent a lot of money buying records and often was a DJ at a friend's party. I never realized that this was his way of avoiding his fear of failing.

Tony

Then, for the second semester of my sophomore year I chose my two regular classes: education and physics. This is where things really got bad.

I always enjoyed math so I felt confident that I'd have no problem with calculus.

I was also looking forward to Physics. I had done well in physics and in AP Physics in high school. But college classes were much harder.

Weekly Physics lab reports were expected to be at least 25-35 pages long, with a whole bunch of statistics and other math I had not learned yet.

I think I understood the Physics at least as much as half the class, if not more, but proving that on paper with lab reports or timed tests never worked for me. I failed the education class and might as well have failed physics because the grade was so low.

That summer, I took calculus and failed. It only took one semester out of CBS before I realized that BU was not for me.

Judy

Tony was not about to give up. He was ready to take physics and calculus again. We suggested he try the University of Massachusetts in Boston. UMass cost less and we hoped the classes might be a little easier

The worst time of my life

While I went to UMass, I lived off campus with my girlfriend and my best friend. Actually, she was more than just a girlfriend. Perhaps I should say, my soulmate. and my very best friend.

I was in love with her and I believed she loved me. I even took her to meet

my parents. I was planning to marry
her and I was happy,

Then, suddenly, **my whole world
crashed around me.**

One Sunday morning my girlfriend
woke up in my bed. That Sunday night
she walked across the hall to my best
friend's bed and that was that.

On Monday night they told me they
were moving out. They left me
all alone and expected me to pay
all the bills.

I called my parents and they tried
to help. They suggested I see a
therapist. I really should have,
but I didn't.

I fell into a depression so deep and
all-consuming that it affected me
for almost ten more years. I couldn't
stop crying.

Tony

My mother recently asked me why I failed calculus and physics again and again. She wondered if I did all the homework.

I really went to all the classes and I did all the homework. I thought for a while that I understood it but I didn't. I should have gotten a tutor but I didn't.

The second time I took physics and calculus, I was overconfident. I thought it would be easier the second time. It wasn't. I don't think it was a reading problem. Even with a third-grade reading level, I think I understood all the questions.

I'm just glad that my parents let me keep trying.

Judy

That summer at UMass, Tony took Physics, Calculus, and a Philosophy class. Somehow, he managed to pass the Philosophy class. He failed calculus and physics.

Tony

I couldn't believe that I kept failing. I knew I was as smart as the other students. I thought it had to be something about dyslexia.

For some reason, none of us seemed to realize that a major reason why I went to all my classes and did all my homework and still failed was probably because the breakup left me so depressed.

The depression I felt repeated the loneliness and fear I have felt most of my life.

Looking back at it all, in **2020,** things seem more clear. In January I started taking anti-anxiety medication.

Now, I see how depressed I was back then. I see now how much of the time I just gave up, how often I stopped trying. I kept failing math and physics because I was deeply depressed.

Curry College

At this point, Tony's parents suggested he try Curry College, just south of Boston. They had a four-year program for dyslexic students. Tony agreed to go there as long as they had a physics major. They did.

Tony

I should have gone to Curry College to begin with. All of the students were dyslexic. All of the teachers were willing to help us. I was able to relax and enjoy my classes;

Judy

At Curry college, Tony was doing well. He passed Calculus and Physics and all his other classes. Now, however, Curry College decided to drop their physics major. What a terrible shock.

Thank goodness, just for Tony, their only physics major, they continued classes until he graduated. This was wonderful. It meant many of his classes included only Tony and his teacher. Tony finally graduated with his degree in physics.

Chapter 13.

Grad School is harder than College

A Masters in Education, is recommended
or required to teach in the public schools.
Curry had a graduate program in education
but there was no help for dyslexic students at
this level. It took Tony a little longer.

Judy

Getting Tony through college wasn't easy.
Getting him through grad school was even
harder. Tony tried to avoid assistance from
others. Thank goodness, he was willing to
accept my help.

Tony

As my mother said, college was hard
enough but grad school was even
worse. First, it was hard not having
the same support system that was
there for me as an undergraduate.

Next, my classes were only about education and not about science.

Grad school was more of an obstacle course than an opportunity for growth and enrichment. Without my parents' support, I probably would have given up.

Judy

Tony had to write an endless number of research papers. There was no way he could do these alone with a third-grade reading level. He came home nearly every weekend so we could work on them together.

We spent a lot of time at the library, copying journal articles for his papers. Back home, I read most of them aloud. Tony told me to circle sections he wanted in his paper.

Next, Tony came up with several topics and possible outlines for his paper. He cut out the quotes he wanted to use and then organized them.

I sat at the computer while Tony dictated his paper, just as he had done when he was in high school. We added quotes at appropriate places.

An important step was revision. I read what I had typed and Tony told me what to change.

Notice that I worked hard to be sure Tony did his own work. I never told him what to write. I was only his secretary – his secretary and cheerleader.

For his Master's Thesis, Tony used much of what he had learned at the workshop with me on Brain-based Learning and Teaching. He then wrote his thesis: *Brain-based Teaching in the physics class.*

Finally, Tony graduated.

Parents and children: Now, looking back, I can see that the worst mistake we made was not understanding that Tony was depressed.

Facing college with a third-grade reading level had to be terrifying. We should have insisted that he see a therapist or a doctor. He would have felt better. He would not have felt that he was a failure. He would have done better in his classes.

The other thing we should have done was encourage him to hire a tutor as soon as He knew a course was difficult. He would have done better in his classes and been able to relax.

Chapter 14

An Amazing Summer

Now, Tony needed to get a job. His mother suggested that he do what she always did when looking for a job. She'd print 100 copies of her resume and go from one school to another leaving a copy of her resume.

Tony printed one resume. He got one interview and they hired him. He was a physics teacher and they are hard to find.

This left him with his summer free. He could have gotten a job but Tony had another idea. He had a science book he'd gotten for Christmas from his uncle. It was *River Out of Eden* by Richard Dawkins and Tony really wanted to read it. He had wanted to read it for a long time.

He didn't have taped books anymore. He was on his own. As he explained it to his parents, he studied the first word and tried to guess what it was. Then he studied the next word. When he finished the sentence, he tried to read it.

With his third-grade reading skills, he recognized some words and tried to sound out others.

One by one, he guessed at the unfamiliar words in the first sentence. If it didn't make sense, he changed some of his guesses. Then he did the same thing for the second sentence and the third.

One sentence at a time, he made his way through the book. Then, he went back to the beginning and started over. Each time he read the book it was easier because he understood what the book was about.

Tony

My mother's brother, Uncle Richard, gave me a book for Christmas, that would transform my life, my understanding of the universe and myself. It was the "River out of Eden" by Richard Dawkins.

It was easy to read because he wrote it for children, or at least young adults. It was about Evolution and I was instantly hooked.

Having read this book, myself, I found the strength and the audacity to read other books of Dawkins: "The Selfish Gene" and "The Blind Watchmaker."

It took me a long time to read each of these books four times but I needed to know what was in those books and just reading each book once wasn't enough.

I cared so much about learning things that matter to me that something seemed to push my anxieties and self-doubt to the side.

Each book I read made it easier to read the next. I went on to read other books including *Guns, Germs and Steel* and *Collapse* by Jared Diamond.

Judy

Another person might not find these books interesting. You need to find books you are really determined to read.

Tony didn't tell us what he was doing. The next time we saw Tony, he was reading a *Scientific*

American. We were shocked. "Can you read that?" we asked.

"Sure," he said.

"I taught myself to read."

Judy tested Tony about a year ago. She was delighted to see that Tony scored above a twelfth-grade reading level. It was true. He really taught himself to read.

While this worked for Tony, it does not mean this would work for others but there certainly is no reason not to try teaching yourself how to read.

Tony

My mother asked if I could only read books about science. I think that's mostly true. Every time I worked hard to read a book it was a science book. Those were the books I really wanted to read. You might say I was desperate to read them.

They were easier for me because I was familiar with scientific vocabulary. I was never interested in history and I don't know their vocabulary so I'd probably find it much harder to read a history book.

Another thing I should say is that even if I taught myself to read, that didn't help me improve my handwriting or my spelling.

I'm sure I have slowly improved in both of these, especially with words I use frequently but I'll never write as well as I'd like.

I am still enjoying my work teaching high school physics. I always let the principal and other teachers know that I'm dyslexic. I tell students too, explaining that they can write and spell better than I can.

I let them know that I don't mind being corrected. My job is teaching them physics (or whatever I happen to be teaching), that I know a lot about the subject and that I will help them learn.

Chapter 15.

Reflections 25 years later

Tony

When I finally started taking anti-anxiety medication. I finally looked back and understood how depressed I was when I was in college.

Most of the time, I felt anxious and worried. I kept going over and over in my head about how I was a failure. I failed at sports, failed with girls, failed at reading, and I'd even failed at living my life.

I was filled with fear, fear of failure and fear of being alone. Sometimes I am surprised I managed to get through it. Sometimes I think I'm still getting through it now.

A Summary of my Life

Now, thinking back, I might have
forgotten the dream I had in the
Marshalls and I might have forgotten
the camp that seemed so terrible,
if nothing else had made me keep
thinking about them.

First and second grade wouldn't
have been that bad if I had ended
up reading as well as the other kids
in my class.

But then, I was more and more aware
that I was different. I was aware that
the other students seemed to think I
was stupid. I was aware that I didn't
have any friends in school. My anxiety
began to grow worse and worse.

When I began going to the special
class for kids with dyslexia, I felt
hopeful at first but when it didn't get
any better, when I still couldn't read,

my anxiety, my feeling that I was a failure at everything, kept growing.

If the best teacher for dyslexic students in all of Brockton couldn't teach me how to read, then that neurologist might have been right. I might never learn to read or write.

When we moved to Rhode Island, when I could do well in classes without needing to read or write, I felt great. I had friends, not a lot of friends, but enough.

I did some things I was really proud of like my science fair projects and teaching my mother's classes. Nobody seemed to think I was stupid but somehow, that feeling that I was a failure stuck with me.

I wasn't as rich as the others. I couldn't read as well as they did. And I was terribly afraid that, in the future, I'd still be a failure.

In high school and then in college, there were some great experiences but I still knew that a third-grade reading level wasn't enough.

I really wanted to be a high school physics teacher, but I kept wondering if you can really teach physics if you can't read the book?

I also knew I'd never make it through high school or college without my mother. My parents were proud of me for not giving up. I'm just glad that my parents didn't give up, that they let me keep trying.

Now, it might sound silly, but my biggest problem is spelling. When I began teaching, I would call parents when there were problems with my students. It was easy to talk to parents on the phone.

Now, sometimes, I'm expected to email parents when there is a problem. Writing an email takes me at least 4-5 times as long as calling a parent and I always feel anxious about my spelling and even my grammar.

I'm careful to spell-check what I write, but sometimes I still end up with the right spelling for the wrong word.

Sometimes I feel an enormous pressure to get it all done fast – to write that email in the same amount of time that others take. Then I get really anxious. Finally, I just block it out and stop thinking about it.

I'm good at that, at blocking out what I can't take, what hurts too much.

Reflections on writing this book together

My mother keeps asking me difficult questions. This time she asked me two questions. First, she wanted me to write a little about writing a book together. Second, she asked me why, until now,

I had never told her or anyone how I really felt.

I tried to pretend I was back in first or second grade. She'd ask me how school was and I think I always said OK, or maybe Good. It wasn't OK and it sure wasn't good, but I didn't know what else to say.

Perhaps, just thinking about how I felt would hurt so I tried not to " think about it. Talking about it would hurt even worse.

In college, I did talk to my parents when my girlfriend and best friend left. I had to talk to someone. I was seriously depressed and probably should have talked to a therapist. But after that, I went back to saying everything was fine – even when it wasn't.

And this brings me to writing this book. I thought writing a book together would be fun. I had lots of interesting stories to tell and, just like my mother, I had images of a simple happy story. But when it came to writing, I couldn't get started.

Finally, when my parents were visiting, Mom cornered me while I was washing dishes. She asked questions and took notes. When she printed up the notes, I read them and sometimes made changes or a few additions.

Finally, I built up my courage a little at a time. I knew she wouldn't complain about my spelling. That wasn't the problem. I was slowly beginning to realize that writing about growing up dyslexic isn't easy. It really is hard.

I'd spent all those years hiding my feelings from them and from myself. Writing my story was painful.

Then, to her surprise and to my surprise, I began writing more and more. I was able to write about the pain I had felt but could never talk or even think about.

Sure, I have bad days – days when I still feel like I'm a failure at everything. A lot of people have bad days. But I also have my good days – even some really great days.

So, what if I was a failure at sports? So was my sister, and my mother and father. But that's not true. None of us were failures. I tried more different sports that the rest of my family put together. I was even on the rugby team at Boston. University until I had a terribly bad leg break and the doctor said no more rugby and no more skiing.

Very few people are great at sports. Sports are meant for fun, not for winning. That means you cannot be a failure in sports. I complain about being a failure at writing. Most people with dyslexia have problems with writing. I'm amazed at how much my writing has improved. I have no reason to be embarrassed.

I really wasn't a failure at girls. Actually, I did pretty well. There was one year when I went to three different high school proms. In college, I had plenty of girlfriends.

I had that one unexpected terrible breakup, but I'm not the only person to have a terrible break-up. In fact, some people go through many terrible break-ups. They may even go through several divorces. Now, I have a wonderful wife and two great sons. I'd have to say I really am a winner.

Was I a failure at college?

It wasn't easy for me. And then, with the breakup it was hard to concentrate. It took me several extra years to finish.

I think of the many students who drop out of college – even out of high school. I refused to give up. I finished high school. I graduated from college with a degree in physics, and a Master's degree in education.

What a fool I am to call that a failure. Anyone else would say that's a success.

Then, there were all those other successes along the way. Teaching my mother's classes about dyslexia, winning awards at the Science Fairs, getting my Eagle in Scouts, teaching at College Academy, and so much more.

And reading? Sure, it took me longer
to learn but there are so many people,
with or without dyslexia, who can't read
nearly as well as I do now.

I am NOT a failure at reading. The
reason we are writing this book is
because I managed, against all odds, to
become a SUCCESS in reading.

I say all this, not to brag about my
success but because I know there are
other people with dyslexia who continue
to believe they are failures.

It's hard, after years of being the only
kid in your class who can't read – to stop
thinking of yourself as a failure.

I think the first time I really felt like
a success was in seventh grade when
I taught my mother's classes about
dyslexia. Those kids told their friends
about me. They looked forward to when
I'd be there the next time.

Some said that their problems weren't
as bad as mine and that if I could go to

college, they could do that too. I had no idea I could inspire students like this.

Then, in that physics class at Landmark, when they said I couldn't take the class because I couldn't read well enough, and then I was selected as one of the two students to take a physics class at Harvard. What a success that was!

Now, working with my mother to share my story, I have another chance to be a success. Perhaps this book will help other dyslexic students understand they also can be a success.

I hope that, as some of you experience the downs and ups of growing up dyslexic, that you can know you are not a failure. You never have been.

The educational system failed us. We who are dyslexic, whether we learned to read or not, can still find our own pathways to success.

So, what do I think about writing a book about my life, alone or with my mother? Either way, it isn't easy. If you are honest, it is painful but, in the end, it feels good, very good.

I'd say it's great to finally be able to understand myself. And about writing the book with my mother, I don't think I could have done it alone. She pushed me a little at a time to write, to write more, and to think about how I felt all those years ago.

The most important parts of the book came when she asked me all those questions, painful questions, questions that made me think, questions that forced me to get past the fences I had put up so I didn't need to think about it anymore.

Thanks Mom, I couldn't have done any of this without you.

Judy

As I reflect on writing together, I know I have learned things about Tony I never would have discovered. Now I know why he couldn't share his feelings. They were too painful. As I read what he wrote, I was in tears.

This has been a painful journey for all of us but it was an important journey. It has helped us both to know ourselves better as well as knowing each other better.

Tony, we began thinking we were writing about only one battle, learning how to read. Now I see that there were three battles. There were also three books.

In elementary school, you fought against the pain of not being able to read or write and of seeing yourself as the only kid in your class who couldn't read.

In middle school, you won that battle with the help of taped books and *The Lord of the*

Rings. You fought that battle yourself and you won.

In high school and college, you recognized that a third-grade reading level wasn't enough. You fought against the ever-present fear of failure.

After grad school, you finally won that battle with another book, the *River out of Eden* by

Richard Dawkins. You no longer needed to fear failure. You really could read.

That's where we thought the story would end but there was a third battle. You still had to deal with the pain that you had kept to yourself all these years. This time the book is *How Tony Learned to Read*. It is this book, the book you have written yourself.

Writing this book had to be terribly difficult. It pushed you to realize that you have been hiding these feelings for all these years and to explain why you couldn't talk about these things before,

It took a great deal of courage to recognize your feelings, fears, and depression. It took courage to share them with your parents and now to share them with the world. Finally, you can say you have won this battle.

You changed this book from a simple feel-good book to a book that reveals what so many dyslexic students hide for the rest of their lives. Thank you, Tony.

Now, I am so pleased to read your final statement. This is the Tony I remember, the Tony who knew he could reach his goals if he

tried hard enough, the Tony who was strong
and brave and who never gave up.

Tony

No longer do I think of giving up.
I don't back down or walk away. I
stand and fight.

I am no longer the boy in his
underwear running in the woods
at night from a monster that was
only in my mind.

I am no longer paralyzed with
anxiety. I feel free – free without
boundaries and I will continue
to fight this fight like it means
my survival.

The End

We are not experts in the field but if you would like to talk to either of us you can email us.

Suggested questions for Book Clubs available. Contact Judy or Tony.

Email Judy at jjfishel@gmail.com

Email Tony at wolftree. fishel@gmail.com

If you enjoyed this book, if you found it helpful, please tell your friends.

The best way to share your opinions of the book is to write a review on Amazon. The more reviews we get, the more people will see the book.

It would also help if you leave a review on your blog, on social media and anywhere else that might reach families with dyslexic children.

We would really appreciate your help.

Author Bios

TONY FISHEL

Tony was eight years old when a neurologist told him he was extremely intelligent but also severely dyslexic and that he might never learn to read or write.

Tony was in about fifth grade when he decided to be a physics teacher.

In college, he failed physics and calculus several time but he didn't give up.

After graduate school, he finally taught himself to read

And yes, he became a high school physics teacher and he has enjoyed teaching in several schools in Massachusetts.

He is married to the love of his life. They live in western Massachusetts with their twins, three cats and a dog.

Tony also enjoys gardening, not finishing projects, and playing records in the basement.

JUDY FISHEL

Judy was a teacher who always focused on the needs of her students more than on the subjects. Most of the time she taught middle or high school math and science. She twice won Presidential Awards for teaching Math.

After retiring, she turned to writing. This is the fourth book she has published:

Her first two books, *Straight A's Are NOT Enough* - first and second editions – are about study skills mainly for college freshmen. They would be helpful for anyone interested in what it means to really study. The second edition would be especially helpful for your student starting in high school.

3. *Murder of the Obeah Man* is a mystery that takes place in Florida and features a Jamaican woman who is an herbalist, healer, spiritual advisor, and wants to help the detectives find the killer.

Color pictures of Tony on Judy's Author Page

Pictures of Tony Growing Up

Tony teaching himself to walk

Tony and his sister in the Philippines

The Marshall Islands Majuro Atoll

ocean and reef – beach – houses - lagoon

Tony plays barefoot on the reef

Tony with his playmates

Graduating from preschool

Climbing half-way up the coconut palm

Tony in elementary school, sister & dog

Tony with planaria science fair project

Tony teaching his mother's class

Tony in high school

Tony's grandpa teaches him in the boat

Tony tenth grade science fair project

Tony Graduates from high school and celebrates with flowers from the garden.

CPSIA information can be obtained
at www.ICGtesting.com
Printed in the USA
LVHW022315220421
685283LV00016B/1024